O'Halloran

by Iain Gray

Lang**Syne**

PUBLISHING

WRITING *to* REMEMBER

LangSyne

PUBLISHING

WRITING *to* REMEMBER

E-mail: info@lang-syne.co.uk

Distributed in the Republic of Ireland by Portfolio Group,
Kilbarrack Ind. Est. Kilbarrack, Dublin 5.
T:00353(01) 839 4918 F:00353(01) 839 5826
sales@portfoliogroup.ie
www.portfoliogroup.ie

Design by Dorothy Meikle   Printed by Martins the Printers

© Lang Syne Publishers Ltd 2011

ISBN 978-1-85217-324-1

O'Halloran

MOTTO:
Clann Fearghaile abú
(Victory to the head of Fearghaile).

CREST:
A lizard.

NAME variations include:
Ó hAllmhuráin (*Gaelic*)
O'Halleron
Haloran
Halleron
Holleran
Holoran
Halloran
Holloron

Chapter one:
Origins of Irish surnames

**According to an old saying, there are two types of Irish –
those who actually are Irish and those who wish they were.**

This sentiment is only one example of the allure that the
high romance and drama of the proud nation's history holds
for thousands of people scattered across the world today.

It's a sad fact, however, that the vast majority of Irish
surnames are found far beyond Irish shores, rather than on
the Emerald Isle itself.

The population stood at around eight million souls in
1841, but today it stands at fewer than six million.

This is mainly a tragic consequence of the potato
famine, also known as the Great Hunger, which devastated
Ireland between 1845 and 1849.

The Irish peasantry had become almost wholly reliant
for basic sustenance on the potato, first introduced from the
Americas in the seventeenth century.

When the crop was hit by a blight, at least 800,000
people starved to death while an estimated two million
others were forced to seek a new life far from their native
shores – particularly in America, Canada, and Australia.

The effects of the potato blight continued until about
1851, by which time a firm pattern of emigration had
become established.

Ireland's loss, however, was to the gain of the countries in which the immigrants settled, contributing enormously, as their descendants do today, to the well being of the nations in which their forefathers settled.

But those who were forced through dire circumstance to establish a new life in foreign parts never forgot their roots, or the proud heritage and traditions of the land that gave them birth.

Nor do their descendants.

It is a heritage that is inextricably bound up in the colourful variety of Irish names themselves – and the origin and history of these names forms an integral part of the vibrant drama that is the nation's history, one of both glorious fortune and tragic misfortune.

This history is well documented, and one of the most important and fascinating of the earliest sources are *The Annals of the Four Masters*, compiled between 1632 and 1636 by four friars at the Franciscan Monastery in County Donegal.

Compiled from earlier sources, and purporting to go back to the Biblical Deluge, much of the material takes in the mythological origins and history of Ireland and the Irish.

This includes tales of successive waves of invaders and settlers such as the Fomorians, the Partholonians, the Nemedians, the Fir Bolgs, the Tuatha De Danann, and the Laigain.

Of particular interest are the *Milesian Genealogies*,

because the majority of Irish clans today claim a descent from either Heremon, Ir, or Heber – three of the sons of Milesius, a king of what is now modern day Spain.

These sons invaded Ireland in the second millennium B.C, apparently in fulfilment of a mysterious prophecy received by their father.

This Milesian lineage is said to have ruled Ireland for nearly 3,000 years, until the island came under the sway of England's King Henry II in 1171 following what is known as the Cambro-Norman invasion.

This is an important date not only in Irish history in general, but for the effect the invasion subsequently had for Irish surnames.

'Cambro' comes from the Welsh, and 'Cambro-Norman' describes those Welsh knights of Norman origin who invaded Ireland.

But they were invaders who stayed, inter-marrying with the native Irish population and founding their own proud dynasties that bore Cambro-Norman names such as Archer, Barbour, Brannagh, Fitzgerald, Fitzgibbon, Fleming, Joyce, Plunkett, and Walsh – to name only a few.

These 'Cambro-Norman' surnames that still flourish throughout the world today form one of the three main categories in which Irish names can be placed – those of Gaelic-Irish, Cambro-Norman, and Anglo-Irish.

Previous to the Cambro-Norman invasion of the twelfth century, and throughout the earlier invasions and settlement of those wild bands of sea rovers known as the Vikings in the eighth and ninth centuries, the population of the island was relatively small, and it was normal for a person to be identified through the use of only a forename.

But as population gradually increased and there were many more people with the same forename, surnames were adopted to distinguish one person, or one community, from another.

Individuals identified themselves with their own particular tribe, or 'tuath', and this tribe – that also became known as a clann, or clan – took its name from some distinguished ancestor who had founded the clan.

The Gaelic-Irish form of the name Kelly, for example, is Ó Ceallaigh, or O'Kelly, indicating descent from an original 'Ceallaigh', with the 'O' denoting 'grandson of.' The name was later anglicised to Kelly.

The prefix 'Mac' or 'Mc', meanwhile, as with the clans of the Scottish Highlands, denotes 'son of.'

Although the Irish clans had much in common with their Scottish counterparts, one important difference lies in what are known as 'septs', or branches, of the clan.

Septs of Scottish clans were groups who often bore an entirely different name from the clan name but were under the clan's protection.

In Ireland, septs were groups that shared the same name and who could be found scattered throughout the four provinces of Ulster, Leinster, Munster, and Connacht.

The 'golden age' of the Gaelic-Irish clans, infused as their veins were with the blood of Celts, pre-dates the Viking invasions of the eighth and ninth centuries and the Norman invasion of the twelfth century, and the sacred heart of the country was the Hill of Tara, near the River Boyne, in County Meath.

Known in Gaelic as 'Teamhar na Rí', or Hill of Kings, it was the royal seat of the 'Ard Rí Éireann', or High King of Ireland, to whom the petty kings, or chieftains, from the island's provinces were ultimately subordinate.

It was on the Hill of Tara, beside a stone pillar known as the Irish 'Lia Fáil', or Stone of Destiny, that the High Kings were inaugurated and, according to legend, this stone would emit a piercing screech that could be heard all over Ireland when touched by the hand of the rightful king.

The Hill of Tara is today one of the island's main tourist attractions.

Opposition to English rule over Ireland, established in the wake of the Cambro-Norman invasion, broke out frequently and the harsh solution adopted by the powerful forces of the Crown was to forcibly evict the native Irish from their lands.

These lands were then granted to Protestant colonists, or 'planters', from Britain.

Many of these colonists, ironically, came from Scotland and were the descendants of the original 'Scotti', or 'Scots', who gave their name to Scotland after migrating there in the fifth century A.D., from the north of Ireland.

Colonisation entailed harsh penal laws being imposed on the majority of the native Irish population, stripping them practically of all of their rights.

The Crown's main bastion in Ireland was Dublin and its environs, known as the Pale, and it was the dispossessed peasantry who lived outside this Pale, desperately striving to eke out a meagre living.

It was this that gave rise to the modern-day expression of someone or something being 'beyond the pale'.

Attempts were made to stamp out all aspects of the ancient Gaelic-Irish culture, to the extent that even to bear a Gaelic-Irish name was to invite discrimination.

This is why many Gaelic-Irish names were anglicised with, for example, and noted above, Ó Ceallaigh, or O'Kelly, being anglicised to Kelly.

Succeeding centuries have seen strong revivals of Gaelic-Irish consciousness, however, and this has led to many families reverting back to the original form of their name, while the language itself is frequently found on the fluent tongues of an estimated 90,000 to 145,000 of the island's population.

Ireland's turbulent history of religious and political strife is one that lasted well into the twentieth century, a landmark century that saw the partition of the island into the twenty-six counties of the independent Republic of

Ireland, or Eire, and the six counties of Northern Ireland, or Ulster.

Dublin, originally founded by Vikings, is now a vibrant and truly cosmopolitan city while the proud city of Belfast is one of the jewels in the crown of Ulster.

It was Saint Patrick who first brought the light of Christianity to Ireland in the fifth century A.D.

Interpretations of this Christian message have varied over the centuries, often leading to bitter sectarian conflict – but the many intricately sculpted Celtic Crosses found all over the island are symbolic of a unity that crosses the sectarian divide.

It is an image that fuses the 'old gods' of the Celts with Christianity.

All the signs from the early years of this new millennium indicate that sectarian strife may soon become a thing of the past – with the Irish and their many kinsfolk across the world, be they Protestant or Catholic, finding common purpose in the rich tapestry of their shared heritage.

Chapter two:

High Kings and Vikings

A clan with roots deeply embedded in the ancient soil of Ireland, the O'Hallorans were from earliest times to be found in what today are the counties of Galway and Clare.

The Gaelic-Irish form of the name is Ó hAllmhuráin, thought to indicate 'from beyond the sea', and it was two separate septs, or branches, of this clan that flourished near Lough Corrib in Galway and on the shore of Lough Derg in the barony of Tulla, in Clare.

In common with the vast majority of native Irish clans the O'Hallorans can trace a proud descent back through the dim mists of time to the island's earliest monarchs.

In the case of the O'Hallorans this is through Heber who, along with Heremon, Ir and Amergin and four other brothers, was a son of Milesius.

A king of what is now modern day Spain, Milesius had planned to invade Ireland in fulfilment of a mysterious Druidic prophecy.

He died before he could embark on the invasion but his sons, including Heber, Ir, Heremon and Amergin, successfully undertook the daunting task in his stead.

Legend holds that their invasion fleet was scattered in a storm and Ir killed when his ship was driven onto the island of Scellig-Mhicheal, off the coast of modern day Co. Kerry.

Only Heremon, Heber, and Amergin survived, although Ir left issue.

Heremon and Heber became the first of the Milesian monarchs of Ireland, but Heremon later killed Heber in a quarrel said to have been caused by their wives, while Amergin was slain by Heremon in an argument over territory.

Along with the O'Hallorans, other clans that trace a descent from Heber include those of Brady, Brennan, Carroll, Casey, Clancy, Doran, Hogan, Kennedy, Lynch, McCarthy, McNamara, O'Brien, O'Callaghan, O'Connor and O'Neill.

The O'Hallorans were also of the tribal grouping known as the Dál Cais, or Dalcassians – named from the legendary Cormac Cas, the early to mid-third century chieftain of the province of Munster who was renowned for his remarkable courage, strength and dexterity.

It was this Cormac Cas who inflicted a celebrated defeat on the men of the province of Leinster in a battle fought near present day Wexford, but was killed in battle in 254 A.D. at Dun-tri-Liag, or the Fort of the Stone Slabs, known today as Duntrileague, in Co. Limerick.

His deathblow, according to the ancient annals, came from the spear of the colourfully named Eochy of the Red Eyebrows, King of Leinster.

But his Dalcassian descendants, who number the

O'Hallorans among their ranks, were destined in later centuries to inflict a resounding defeat on invaders from across the sea.

It was in the closing years of the eighth century A.D. that the sinister longboats of the fierce Scandinavian sea rovers more commonly known as the Vikings first appeared off Irish shores – and one of their first acts was to loot and burn the monastery of St. Patrick's Island, near Skerries in present day Co. Dublin, to the ground.

Raids continued along the coastline until they made their first forays inland in 836 A.D., while a year later a Viking fleet of 60 vessels sailed into the River Boyne.

An indication of the terror they brought can be found in one contemporary account of their depredations and desecrations.

It lamented how 'the pagans desecrated the sanctuaries of God, and poured out the blood of saints upon the altar, laid waste the house of our hope, trampled on the bodies of saints in the temple of God, like dung in the street.'

By 841 A.D. the Vikings, or Ostmen as they were also known, had established a number of strongholds on the island, but their raids began to ease off before returning with a terrifying and bloody vengeance in about 914 A.D.

They met with a determined resistance from the native Irish, most notably in the form of the forces of the powerful confederation of clans known as the southern Uí Neill.

The Irish suffered a resounding defeat at the battle of

Dublin in 919 A.D., and it was not until just over thirty years later that the raids gradually came to an end.

Having putting aside the broadsword and battleaxe in favour of the more peaceful pursuit of trade, the Vikings contributed significantly to Ireland's fortunes by, for example, establishing Dublin as a main European trading port.

By 1002 A.D. the Dalcassian leader Brian Bóruma, better known to posterity as Brian Boru, had achieved the prize of the High Kingship of Ireland – but there were still rival chieftains, and not least the Vikings, to deal with.

He was able to achieve this by managing to rally a number of other chieftains to his cause, but by no means all.

Boru, ancestor of the distinguished O'Brien clan, had achieved the High Kingship with his battle-hardened warriors known as the Dalcassian knights at his side.

But, resenting his kingship, a number of chieftains found common cause with the Vikings, and the two sides met in final and bloody confrontation at the battle of Clontarf, about four miles north of Dublin, on Good Friday, 1014.

Boru and his Dalcassian warriors, who included O'Hallorans, proved victorious, but the annals speak of great slaughter on the day, with the dead piled high on the field of battle, while hundreds of Vikings drowned as they sought the safety of their ships.

Among the many dead were Brian Boru's three sons, Murrough, Conaing and Moltha.

Boru, meanwhile, had little time to celebrate his victory – being killed in his tent by a party of fleeing Vikings led by Brodar the Dane.

The first to enter the tent had his legs cut off with one sweep of Boru's mighty two-handed sword.

Brodar then struck him a fatal blow on the back of his head with his axe, but he rallied the last of his dying strength to cut off his assailant's head with another vicious sweep of his sword before killing yet another Viking.

Brian Boru and all who fought for him at the battle of Clontarf passed into legend, and the great warrior king was buried in a stone coffin on the north side of the high altar in Armagh Church.

Described by a number of sources as being 'of the same stock' as their fellow Dalcassians the McNamaras, the Clare sept of the O'Hallorans found both their glorious fortunes and tragic misfortunes closely allied to those of the McNamaras.

One indication of the possible genealogical link between the two clans can be found in the fact that the Gaelic-Irish form of the O'Halloran name, as noted above, translates as 'from beyond the sea', while the Gaelic-Irish form of McNamara – MacConmara – stems from 'Conmara', meaning 'hound of the sea.'

Meanwhile the O'Halloran motto of 'Clann Fearghaile abú', translated as 'Victory to the head of Fearghaile', originates from the Galway sept of the family.

With 'Fearghaile' denoting 'man of valour', this may suggest an admittedly tenuous link with the clan of Ó Fearghaile, or O'Farrell.

Back on the field of battle, Brian Boru's success in uniting the Dalcassians and inflicting defeat on the Vikings at the battle of Clontarf does not imply that the Dalcassian clans were always united.

In common with other clans scattered throughout the four ancient provinces of Ulster, Leinster, Munster and Connacht, they frequently found themselves engaged in bitter conflict with one another.

In the case of the O'Hallorans and the McNamaras of Clare this was mainly through alliance with the more powerful O'Briens against clans such as the O'Gradys and others.

It was this disunity that worked to the advantage of a later wave of invaders, who descended on the island in all their disciplined and armoured might in the late twelfth century.

Chapter three:

Under the yoke

Far from being a unified nation, the Ireland of the twelfth century was split into territories ruled over by proud and ambitious chieftains who ruled as kings in their own right.

In a series of bloody conflicts, one chieftain, or king, would occasionally gain the upper hand over his rivals, and by 1156 the most powerful was Muirchertach MacLochlainn, King of the O'Neills.

The equally powerful Rory O'Connor, King of the province of Connacht, opposed him but he increased his power and influence by allying himself with Dermot MacMurrough, King of Leinster.

MacLochlainn and MacMurrough were aware that the main key to the kingdom of Ireland was the thriving trading port of Dublin and their combined forces managed to seize it.

But when MacLochlainn died the Dubliners rose up in revolt and overthrew the unpopular MacMurrough.

A triumphant Rory O'Connor then entered Dublin and was inaugurated as Ard Rí, but the proud Dermott MacMurrough was not one to humbly accept defeat.

He appealed for help from England's Henry II in unseating O'Connor, an act that was to radically affect the future course of Ireland's fortunes.

The English monarch agreed to help MacMurrough, but distanced himself from direct action by delegating his Norman subjects in Wales with the task.

These ambitious and battle-hardened barons and knights had first settled in Wales following the Norman Conquest of England in 1066 and, with an eye on rich booty, plunder, and lands, were only too eager to obey their sovereign's wishes and furnish MacMurrough with aid.

MacMurrough crossed the Irish Sea to Bristol, where he rallied powerful barons such as Robert Fitzstephen and Maurice Fitzgerald to his cause, along with Gilbert de Clare, Earl of Pembroke.

The mighty Norman war machine soon moved into action, and so fierce and disciplined was their onslaught on the forces of Rory O'Connor and his allies that by 1171 they had recaptured Dublin, in the name of MacMurrough, and other strategically important territories.

Henry II now began to have second thoughts over the venture, aware that he may have ultimately been responsible for the creation of a rival in the form of a separate Norman kingdom in Ireland.

He landed on the island, near Waterford, at the head of a large army with the aim of curbing the power of his barons, but protracted war was averted when the barons submitted to the royal will, promising homage and allegiance in return for holding the territories they had conquered in the king's name.

Henry also received the submission and homage of many of the Irish chieftains, tired as they were with internecine warfare and also perhaps realising that as long as they were rivals and not united they were no match for the powerful forces the English Crown could muster.

English dominion over Ireland was later ratified through the Treaty of Windsor of 1175, under the terms of which Rory O'Connor, for example, was only allowed to rule territory unoccupied by the Normans in the role of a vassal of the king.

But the land was far from settled, blighted as it was with years of warfare and smarting under many grievances.

There were actually three separate Irelands.

These were the territories of the privileged and powerful Norman barons and their retainers and the Ireland of the disaffected Gaelic-Irish such as the O'Hallorans who held lands unoccupied by the Normans.

Then there was the grimly named Pale – comprised of Dublin itself and a substantial area of its environs ruled over by an English elite.

It was not long before Ireland was under the yoke of an oppression that was directed in the main against native Irish clans such as the O'Hallorans.

An indication of the harsh treatment meted out to them can be found in a desperate plea sent to Pope John XII by Roderick O'Carroll of Ely, Donald O'Neill of Ulster, and a number of other Irish chieftains in 1318.

They stated: 'As it very constantly happens, whenever an Englishman, by perfidy or craft, kills an Irishman, however noble, or however innocent, be he clergy or layman, there is no penalty or correction enforced against the person who may be guilty of such wicked murder.

'But rather the more eminent the person killed and the higher rank which he holds among his own people, so much more is the murderer honoured and rewarded by the English, and not merely by the people at large, but also by the religious and bishops of the English race.'

This appeal to the Pope had no effect whatsoever in alleviating the plight of the native Irish.

Their situation deteriorated further through a policy of 'plantation', or settlement of loyal Protestants on land held by the native Irish.

This policy started during the reign from 1491 to 1547 of Henry VIII, whose Reformation effectively outlawed the established Roman Catholic faith throughout his dominions, and continued throughout the subsequent reigns of Elizabeth I and James I, and in the wake of the Cromwellian invasion of 1649.

This Cromwellian invasion came in the aftermath of a rebellion that broke out in 1641 and whose consequences still resonate throughout the island today.

In the insurrection that exploded, at least 2,000 Protestant settlers were massacred at the hands of Catholic landowners and their native Irish peasantry, while thousands more were stripped of their belongings and driven from their lands to seek refuge where they could.

Terrible as the atrocities against the Protestant settlers were, subsequent accounts became greatly exaggerated, serving to fuel a burning desire for revenge.

Tragically for Ireland, this revenge became directed not only against the rebels in particular but native Irish Catholics such as the O'Hallorans in general.

The English Civil War intervened to prevent immediate action against the rebels, but following the execution of Charles I in 1649 and the consolidation of the power of England's Oliver Cromwell, the time was ripe for revenge.

The Lord Protector, as he was named, descended on Ireland at the head of a 20,000-strong army that landed at Ringford, near Dublin, in August of 1649.

He had three main aims.

These were to quash all forms of rebellion, to 'remove' all Catholic landowners who had taken part in the rebellion, and to convert the native Irish to the Protestant faith.

An early warning of the terrors that were in store came when Drogheda was stormed and taken in September and between 2,000 and 4,000 of its inhabitants killed, including priests who were summarily put to the sword.

The defenders of Drogheda's St. Peter's Church, who had refused to surrender, were burned to death as they huddled for refuge in the steeple and the church was deliberately torched.

A similar fate awaited Wexford, on the southeast coast, when at least 1,500 of its inhabitants were slaughtered, including 200 defenceless women, despite their pathetic pleas for mercy.

Cromwell soon held the benighted land in a grip of iron, allowing him to implement what amounted to a policy of ethnic cleansing.

His troopers were given free rein to hunt down and kill priests, while Catholic landholdings such as those of the O'Hallorans were confiscated, and an edict issued stating that any native Irish found east of the River Shannon after May 1, 1654, faced either summary execution or transportation to the West Indies.

Further rebellions occurred in 1668 and in 1798 – all of which led to many native Irish such as the O'Hallorans being forced to leave their native land – with a further emigration during the famine known as The Great Hunger, caused by a failure of the potato crop between 1845 and 1849.

But Ireland's loss of sons and daughters such as the O'Hallorans was to the gain of those far-flung countries in which they settled, with one of the many examples being Joseph O'Halloran, who was born in Clare in 1718 and went on to hold the prestigious post of professor of surgery at the University of Bordeaux, in France.

Chapter four:

On the world stage

From acting and sport to politics and literature, bearers of the O'Halloran name, in all its rich variety of spellings, have achieved fame in a diverse array of pursuits and callings.

Born in 1969 in Manhattan, **Brian O'Halloran** is the American actor who is best known for his *Clerks* series of films from the 1990s, while he also appeared in the 1995 *Mallrats* and the 2008 *The Happening*.

A former boxer who fought under the name of Irish Jack O'Halloran, **Jack O'Halloran** is the American actor who was born in 1943 in Philadelphia.

As a heavyweight boxer from 1966 until his retiral from the ring in 1974, he went undefeated through his first sixteen professional fights.

Moving from the boxing ring to the stage, his first film role was as Moose Malloy in the 1975 *Farewell, My Lovely*, starring Robert Mitchum, while his most famous roles are as the super-villain Non in the 1978 *Superman* and the 1980 *Superman II*.

In the highly competitive world of sport **Shawn Halloran** is the former American football quarterback star who was born in 1964 in Gardner, Massachusetts.

Formerly a player for the Boston College Eagles and the

St. Louis Cardinals, at the time of writing he holds the prestigious post of assistant coach for Yale University.

In European football, **Keith O'Halloran**, born in 1975 in Dublin, is the Irish professional right-winger who began his career in 1994 with English team Middlesborough and who has since played for teams that include Scottish club St. Johnstone and Irish club Shamrock Rovers.

Another leading Republic of Ireland footballer is **Greg O'Halloran**, born in 1980 in Cork.

Teams he has played for include Galway United and Hull City while, at the time of writing, he plays for Cobh Ramblers in the Irish national league.

In the swimming pool, **Kevin O'Halloran** was the top Australian swimmer who was born in 1937 in Katanning, Western Australia, and who died in 1976.

A freestyle swimmer of the 1950s, he won a gold medal in the 4x200-metres freestyle relay at the 1956 Olympics in Melbourne – making him the first Western Australian to win an Olympic gold medal.

A lawyer, politician and businessman, **James O'Halloran** was born in 1820 in Co. Cork, later immigrating with his family to Canada when aged eight.

Studying law at the University of Vermont, he served in the U.S. Army during the war with Mexico before returning to Lower Canada in 1849.

Admitted to the bar in 1852, he set up a legal practice in Cowansville and was later elected as member for

Missisquoi for the Legislative Assembly of the Province of Canada.

Named as a Queen's Counsel in 1864, he later helped to establish the forerunner of the Canadian Pacific Railway known as the South Eastern Railway, and became its first president.

Born in 1893 in Yanyarrie, South Australia, **Michael O'Halloran** was the colourful Australian Labor Party politician who, before his death in 1960, had served in the Australian Senate and as opposition leader in South Australia.

A pioneering Irish trades unionist, **William O'Halloran** was born in 1870 in Co. Galway.

Working on the docks, and in the face of strong opposition from employers, he was instrumental in the foundation of the Galway Workers and General Labourers Union.

His popularity among ordinary folk saw him being elected as Galway City's first Labour councillor in 1914 – but he all but disappeared from political and public life following his active opposition to recruitment into the British Army during the First World War.

In the creative world of music, **Jack Halloran** was the American composer and choral director who was born in 1916 in Rock Rapids, Iowa, and who died in 1997.

He first became popular through the Jack Halloran Quintet, appearing on a number of American television shows, but it was as a choral director for Hollywood films, television shows and music recordings that he became best known.

It was in this capacity that he worked for leading entertainers who included Pat Boone, Ray Charles, Frank Sinatra, Roy Rogers and Dean Martin, while he also served as a president of the American Federation of Television and Radio Artists.

In the world of literature, **Andrew Holleran** is the pseudonym of the acclaimed contemporary American writer Eric Garber, born in 1944.

An essayist, short story writer, novelist and teacher of creative writing at American University in Washington D.C., his novels include the 1978 *Dancer from the Dance*, the 1983 *Nights in Arabia*, the 1996 *The Beauty of Men* and, from 2006, *Grief: A Novel*.

At times a sailor, poet, naval chaplain, forger, journalist and schoolteacher, **Laurence Halloran** certainly lived an interesting life.

Born in Ireland's Co. Meath in 1765, he was orphaned at an early age and placed in the care of an uncle.

He joined the British Royal Navy at the age of 16 – but was imprisoned only a short time later for two years after an altercation in which he stabbed a fellow midshipman to death.

Released from prison, he somehow managed to become headmaster of the respectable Alphington Academy near

Exeter, in England, and came to public notice through the publication in 1790 of his *Odes, Poems and Translations* and, a year later, with his *Poems on Various Occasions*.

By 1805, despite his previous disgrace while serving with the Royal Navy, he had become a naval chaplain – serving aboard the warship Britannia during the famous battle of Trafalgar.

Ever restless, by 1811 he had left the Royal Navy and become rector of the English grammar school at the Cape of Good Hope – but incurred the wrath of fellow colonists by publishing a biting satire on their privileged lifestyles.

Banished from the colony, he returned to Britain in 1818 only to be sentenced shortly afterwards to seven years transportation to Australia after being found guilty of forging coinage.

Curbing his restless and rebellious spirit, he was eventually granted permission to settle in Sydney, where he not only established a weekly newspaper known as *The Gleaner*, but also a school. He died in 1831.

Born in India in 1797, the son of Major General Sir Joseph O'Halloran, **Thomas O'Halloran** settled in Australia in 1838 after following in his father's footsteps and serving with the British Army.

He became the first police commissioner and first police magistrate of South Australia, while the modern day Adelaide suburb of O'Halloran Hill, where he set up a farm known as Lizard Lodge, is named after him.

Meanwhile Halloran is also the name of a suburb of the Central Coast region of Australia's New South Wales, while Halloran Springs is a community in San Bernardino County, California.

Ending on a decidedly spooky note, **Father Walter Halloran** was the Jesuit Roman Catholic priest who became internationally known for his part in the exorcism of a thirteen-year-old boy.

Born in 1921 in Jackson, Minnesota, it was in 1947, while training for the priesthood, that he assisted Father William S. Bowden in the exorcism of a boy from St. Louis, Missouri, who had apparently become possessed by demons after using an Ouija Board.

Father Bowden had asked Halloran to hold the boy down as he performed the complex rite of exorcism – but the boy struck out and broke the priest's nose.

Ordained as a priest in 1954, Father Halloran later recalled how he had seen words written on the boy's body, including 'hell', and how his bed had jumped violently up and down and a bottle of holy water inexplicably smashed against a wall.

It was this exorcism case that inspired the author William Peter Blatty to write the best-selling novel *The Exorcist*, later spine-chillingly adapted for the screen.

Father Halloran, who served as a U.S. paratroops' chaplain from 1969 to 1971 during the Vietnam War, earning two Bronze Stars, died in 2005.

Key dates in Ireland's history from the first settlers to the formation of the Irish Republic:

circa 7000 B.C.	Arrival and settlement of Stone Age people.
circa 3000 B.C.	Arrival of settlers of New Stone Age period.
circa 600 B.C.	First arrival of the Celts.
200 A.D.	Establishment of Hill of Tara, Co. Meath, as seat of the High Kings.
circa 432 A.D.	Christian mission of St. Patrick.
800-920 A.D.	Invasion and subsequent settlement of Vikings.
1002 A.D.	Brian Boru recognised as High King.
1014	Brian Boru killed at battle of Clontarf.
1169-1170	Cambro-Norman invasion of the island.
1171	Henry II claims Ireland for the English Crown.
1366	Statutes of Kilkenny ban marriage between native Irish and English.
1529-1536	England's Henry VIII embarks on religious Reformation.
1536	Earl of Kildare rebels against the Crown.
1541	Henry VIII declared King of Ireland.
1558	Accession to English throne of Elizabeth I.
1565	Battle of Affane.
1569-1573	First Desmond Rebellion.
1579-1583	Second Desmond Rebellion.
1594-1603	Nine Years War.
1606	Plantation' of Scottish and English settlers.

1607	Flight of the Earls.
1632-1636	Annals of the Four Masters compiled.
1641	Rebellion over policy of plantation and other grievances.
1649	Beginning of Cromwellian conquest.
1688	Flight into exile in France of Catholic Stuart monarch James II as Protestant Prince William of Orange invited to take throne of England along with his wife, Mary.
1689	William and Mary enthroned as joint monarchs; siege of Derry.
1690	Jacobite forces of James defeated by William at battle of the Boyne (July) and Dublin taken.
1691	Athlone taken by William; Jacobite defeats follow at Aughrim, Galway, and Limerick; conflict ends with Treaty of Limerick (October) and Irish officers allowed to leave for France.
1695	Penal laws introduced to restrict rights of Catholics; banishment of Catholic clergy.
1704	Laws introduced constricting rights of Catholics in landholding and public office.
1728	Franchise removed from Catholics.
1791	Foundation of United Irishmen republican movement.
1796	French invasion force lands in Bantry Bay.
1798	Defeat of Rising in Wexford and death of United Irishmen leaders Wolfe Tone and Lord Edward Fitzgerald.

1800	Act of Union between England and Ireland.
1803	Dublin Rising under Robert Emmet.
1829	Catholics allowed to sit in Parliament.
1845-1849	The Great Hunger: thousands starve to death as potato crop fails and thousands more emigrate.
1856	Phoenix Society founded.
1858	Irish Republican Brotherhood established.
1873	Foundation of Home Rule League.
1893	Foundation of Gaelic League.
1904	Foundation of Irish Reform Association.
1913	Dublin strikes and lockout.
1916	Easter Rising in Dublin and proclamation of an Irish Republic.
1917	Irish Parliament formed after Sinn Fein election victory.
1919-1921	War between Irish Republican Army and British Army.
1922	Irish Free State founded, while six northern counties remain part of United Kingdom as Northern Ireland, or Ulster; civil war up until 1923 between rival republican groups.
1949	Foundation of Irish Republic after all remaining constitutional links with Britain are severed.